NOTES *from the*

COMMONPLACE BOOK

of a

LEGAL
ANTIQUARIAN

NOTES *from the*
COMMONPLACE BOOK
of a
LEGAL
ANTIQUARIAN

M.H. HOEFLICH

TALBOT
PUBLISHING
Clark, New Jersey

TALBOT PUBLISHING

AN IMPRINT OF

THE LAWBOOK EXCHANGE, LTD.

33 Terminal Avenue
Clark, New Jersey 07066-1321

Please see our website for a selection of our other publications
and fine facsimile reprints of classic works of legal history:
www.lawbookexchange.com

Library of Congress Cataloging-in-Publication Data

Names: Hoeflich, Michael H., compiler.
Title: Notes from the commonplace book of a legal antiquarian / [compiled by] M.H. Hoeflich.
Description: First edition. | Clark, New Jersey : Talbot Publishing, [2021] | Includes bibliographical references. | Summary: "A curated selection of poetry and prose on lawyers and lawyering"-- Provided by publisher.
Identifiers: LCCN 2021055026 | ISBN 9781616196622 (paperback ; acid-free paper)
Subjects: LCSH: Commonplace books. | Lawyers--Miscellanea. | Law--Miscellanea.
Classification: LCC PN6245 .H64 2021 | DDC 808.8/03554--dc23/eng/20211221
LC record available at https://lccn.loc.gov/2021055026

Printed in the United States of America on acid-free paper

For Ross and Steve, who continue to challenge me intellectually, and for Bill, Tom, and Bruce who have been my friends and trusted companions for so long. Without them neither this pamphlet nor its author would exist.

Introduction

When I was young, my family did not have much money and books were things that one borrowed from a library. Early on I discovered that I loved books and the knowledge that they contained, and I was unsatisfied with the temporary possession afforded by library borrowing. This was a serious dilemma for me: I could not afford to buy books but passionately wanted to own books. I was too fearful of punishment to follow Abbie Hoffman's solution to his dilemma of this sort and adopt the life of a book thief.[1] A workable solution to this problem presented itself when I was given a copy of Dag Hammerskjold's *Markings* as an award for excelling in a class at school.[2] Hammerskjold's collection of extracts from his diaries gave me what, I thought, was a brilliant idea: I would be like a diarist yet without recording actions in my daily life; rather I would record a much greater adventure by recording extracts from books I read, the prose of which I wanted to keep nearby.

As the whole of this chapbook attests, I had naively and unknowingly reinvented the commonplace book and commenced a practice that would fascinate me ever since. Indeed, this is not my first time to write of commonplace books or common-placing. And, the study of others'

---

1   Abbie Hoffman, a popular counterculture celebrity in the 1960s was the author of the notorious *Steal This Book* (1971).

2   Dag Hammerskjold, *Markings* (N.Y., 1964). This volume also introduced me to the writings of one of the twentieth century's great poets, W.H. Auden, a friend of Hammerskjold's who wrote its preface.

commonplace endeavors has often informed my more general writings in history.[3]

But at its start, my great, supposed invention was a device by which my impecunious self could build my own library of writings that I could have never otherwise purchased. Looking back at my notes on the texts and my excerpts from the passages I'd found most attractive, I could both revive my memories and retain the use of the contents of the many books that had made the trip from the public library to my apartment and then back again.

In this way, my early habit of collecting quotations from others' writings gave me, at first, both the sense of ownership and the gift of ready and recurrent access to the texts I suddenly "owned." But with age, opportunity, and the good luck that comes of a professional income, common-placing acquired a new and more enduring role in my life. Being one of the most disorganized of human beings, I discovered that, if I found a passage in a book that I wanted to remember—because I found it interesting or because I believed I might use it in my own writings in the future—I should write the passage down in my notebooks. I knew that my future likelihood of finding the one volume that contained that single passage was chancy at best unless I memorialized it in one of my commonplace books. And so my common-placing came to be like the kite string Tom Sawyer used when he and Becky Thatcher were lost in a Missouri cave; it let me trace my way back to the start of every one of my meandering reads.[4]

---

3   M.H. Hoeflich, "The Lawyer as Pragmatic Reader: The History of Legal Common-Placing," *University of Arkansas Law Review*, v. 55 (2002-2003), pp. 53ff.

4   Mark Twain, The Adventures of Tom Sawyer, chapter 31 (1876).

A commonplace book is only as good as the sources from which the entries are drawn. In the case of my commonplace volumes—as you'll see from the extracts in this chapbook—my sources were usually antiquarian books, particularly rare law books. A few years after acquiring my habit of common-placing, I fell prey to an even greater obsession, one distinct from the first even if the two are intricately related. I am, indeed, an obsessive collector of aged and esoteric writings, a habit I might conveniently justify by my study of such writings for the particular style of scholarship I prefer. Yet a more honest admission about my habit would be rooted less in scholarly purpose and more in the accident of a found aesthetic.

I can date the onset of my obsession to the fall of 1969, when I entered Haverford College as a freshman and encountered Richard Luman, a professor who would become one of my greatest friends and mentors. Richard, a brilliant historian who read multiple languages, was an obsessive book collector. His house, just off campus, was less a house than a library with a kitchen attached. Every wall was covered in floor-to-ceiling bookshelves containing thousands of volumes. Most of these were new books, scholarly tomes and large-format volumes on medieval art. But scattered among these new books were a few antiquarian volumes that Richard had picked up over the years. I was enthralled by these aged volumes—their odd sizes, comforting textures, stark images ... even their smell ... the smell of history itself.

The sensory impressions of Richard's ancient pages are still vivid to me, as is my recollection of an immediate desire to acquire some for myself. There was something about these older volumes that simply "spoke" to me. I remember in particular one seventeenth-century volume of Papal biographies filled with woodcut portraits and

Latin texts. When Richard first let me hold this leather covered and gilt decorated folio, I was in love. I loved the feel of the book, the sense of its antiquity, the mystery of who had held it before me, as well as the stories of individuals long gone. In that moment I was reborn as a bibliophile and collector of texts.

Soon I discovered the rare book room at Haverford and then the magnificent Goodhart incunabula collection at Bryn Mawr down the road.[5] It was not long before I took the Paoli Local, the commuter train from Haverford into Philadelphia, to explore the rare books at the University of Pennsylvania library. It was there that a kindly soul—surely not realizing the profound influence her advice would have on my life—told me that while I was in Philadelphia, I should visit William H. Allen's bookstore.[6] I followed her advice. I can still close my eyes and see Walnut Street and the Allen shop ensconced therein. One would enter the store and be confronted with a tsunami of books: they were everywhere, climbing the walls up to the ceiling, filling every nook and cranny. The smell of leather and old paper was overwhelming and intoxicating.

More than forty years and 20,000 volumes later, I live happily surrounded by books and ephemera. Many of these are law books, and many of these venerable tomes are now all but forgotten by the world. Over the past four decades I have taken immense delight in the contents of these books. A continued aspect of this delight has been to collect what I believed were the finest ideas and most evocative prose,

---

5   See, Phyllis W.G. Gordan, "The Medieval Library at Bryn Mawr," *The Papers of the Bibliographical Society of America*, v. 46 (1952), pp. 87ff.

6   See, George H. Allen, *History of William H. Allen Bookseller, 1918-1997*, online at https://www.sas.upenn.edu/~traister/george.html.

along with my impressions at the time, into my notebooks.

Hence, today I have several shelves filled with what I refer to as my commonplace books, filled with choice texts—and the occasional image. By now, kind reader, you will be unsurprised to learn that I have drawn each of the extracts herein from these volumes.

Several years ago, doctors predicted that some irritating health issues would worsen and that, in the then-near future, I would use a wheelchair to move about. They were right, and many of the consequences of the truth of their predictions have been more than irritating. But not all.

One of the advantages of losing one's ability to walk is that it means that one has a great deal of time to read and write. This pamphlet is one positive issue of my present illness. Some years ago, I conceived the idea of putting together a small volume of extracts from my commonplace books. I know the publishing market too well to expect that such a text would ever be given space in the windows at the local Barnes & Noble. I just wanted to make a few of my cherished little extracts available to my friends and colleagues. The book in your hands, dear reader, is the realization of that idea.

There is neither rhyme nor reason to the choice of the extracts included in this pamphlet, other than that they caught my fancy and I wished to preserve them for future entertainment and enlightenment. This selection from my earlier selections for personal use, the *summa summis*, as it were, has as its sole purpose my hope that these texts which have provided me with much pleasure over the years may now do the same for you. Thus, I make this chapbook available to my friends—and I consider anyone who reads this small volume a friend—in the hope that it will provide you a pleasant winter's entertainment. In my mind's eye, these words are reflected up to you by flickering candlelight, while you nestle into a comfortable old chair and sit between the hearth with its warming fire and a sturdy side table with a plate of biscuits and Stilton and a glass of a fine vintage port. Enjoy!

October 2021
Lecompton, Kansas

I

According to an entry in the "Register of Deaths" included in the American Register for 1807, the antebellum American taste for reading Sir William Blackstone's Commentaries on the Laws of England extended well beyond students of the law and practicing lawyers.[7]

Thomas Lungley, born in England, came to Pennsylvania "with a handsome fortune" and became a successful merchant in Upper Makefield, now part of Bucks County. Unfortunately, after some years, Lungley "fell into a partial derangement" and began to pronounce himself to be the "King of Pennsylvania" to anyone who would hear him. He did not insist on any royal prerogatives, however. He did give up his successful business and family, packed a bag with clothing and tools and took to the road working as an "itinerant cooper." His obituarist noted that that he also took to knitting his own socks and repairing his own clothing in a "substantial and workmanlike manner," an activity somewhat unusual for a man at that time and, obviously, worth mentioning in his death notice.

He travelled extensively during this period of his life, including to South Carolina, where, his obituarist noted, that he may have carried on "some secret business, perhaps, with the governor of the state." Apparently, it was near to this time that he also began to say what he called his devotions, "an odd mixture of unconnected sentences,

---

7   M.H. Hoeflich, "American Blackstones," in W. Prest, ed., *Blackstone & his Commentaries: Biography, Law, History* (2009), 171-184.

expressive of no idea nor object...the constancy in the performance of which [he believed] was the only effectual means of preserving Great Britain from foreign invasion." This would seem to indicate that Lungley's derangement did not decrease as time passed.

While these details of Lungley's life after his mental derangement have some human interest and even entertainment value for the modern reader and student of the foibles of human character, it is his reading habits during these later, deranged years of his life that are of particular interest to the legal antiquarian:

> He read with laborious attention judge Blackstone's commentaries on the laws of England, and also Gibson's Treatise on Surveying, and derived therefrom a good degree of valuable improvement in these abstruse sciences.

In this comment we find confirmation that the notion of the law as a "mysterious" or abstruse science was sufficiently widespread in the early American Republic to find its way into an obituary.[8] The second issue, perhaps the more interesting—is whether the reading of Blackstone's *Commentaries* was a cause of Lungley's mental illness or a result thereof. That is likely a question the answer to which will remain forever hidden in the mists of time.

Extract from the American Register (1808 for 1807), p. 74.

---

8   See, D. Boorstin, *The Mysterious Science of Law* (1941).

II

A RECKONING WITH TIME

I.

COME on, old TIME! —nay, that is stuff;
Gaffer! thou comest on fast enough; —
Wing'd foe to feather'd Cupid! —
But, tell me, Sand-Man! ere thy grains
Have multiplied upon my brains,
So thick to make me stupid; —

II.

Tell me, Death's Journeyman! —but, no;
Hear thou my speech; —I will not grow
Irreverent while I try it;
For, though I mock thy Flight, 'tis said,
The Forelock fills me with such dread,
I —*never take thee by it.*

III.

List, then, old Is-Was-and-To-Be!
I'll state accounts 'twixt Thee and Me; —
Thou gavest me, first, the measles;
With *teething* wouldst have ta'en me off,
Then, made'st me, with the hooping cough,
Thinner than fifty weasels.

IV.

Thou gave'st Small-Pox, (the Dragon, now,
That Jenner combats, on a Cow;)
And, then, some seeds of knowledge; —
Grains of the Grammar, which the flails
Of Pedants thresh upon our tails,
To fit us for a College.

V.

And, when at Christ-Church, 'twas thy sport
To rack my brains with sloe-juice Port,
And Lectures out of number! —
There Fresh-man Folly quaffs, and sings,
While Graduate Dulness clogs thy wings,
With mathematick lumber.

VI.

Thy pinions next, —which, while they wave,
Fan all our Birth-Days to the grave, —
I think ere it was prudent,
Balloon'd me from the Schools to Town,
Where I was *parachuted* down,
A dapper, Temple Student.

VII.

Then much in Dramas did I look;
Much slighted Thee, and great Lord Coke;
Congreve beat Blackstone hollow;
Shakspeare made all the Statutes stale,
And, in *my* Crown, no Pleas had Hale,
To supersede Apollo.

VIII.

Ah, Time! those raging heats, I find,
Were the mere Dog-Star of my mind;
    How cool is retrospection!
Youth's gaudy Summer Solstice o'er,
Experience yields a mellow store,
    An Autumn of reflection!

IX.

Why did I let the God of Song
Lure me from Law, to join his throng, —
    Gull'd by some slight applauses?
What's Verse to A when *versus* B?
Or what John Bull, a Comedy,
    To pleading John's Bull's causes?

X.

Yet, though my childhood felt disease,
Though my lank purse, unswol'n by fees,
    Some ragged Muse has netted, —
Still, honest Chronos! 'tis most true,
To Thee (and faith to *others*, too!)
    I'm very much indebted.

XI.

Something made me gaily tough;
Inured me to each day that's rough,
    In hopes of calm, to-morrow; —
And when, old Mower of us all!
Beneath thy sweeping scythe I fall,
    Some *few* dear friends will sorrow.

XII.
Then, —though my idle Prose, or Rhime,
Should, half an hour, out-live me, Time!
Pray bid the Stone-Engravers,
Where'er my bones find Church-Yard room,
Simply to chisel on my tomb, —
"Thank TIME for all his Favours!"

Extract from George Coleman, the Younger,
Poetical vagaries; containing An ode to We,
a hackney'd critick; Low ambition, or The
life and death of Mr. Daw; A reckoning
with time; The lady of the wreck, or Castle
Blarneygig; and Two parsons, or The tale of
a shirt (London, 1814), pp. 17–22.

III

A proclamation was issued on the 6th of November, in the twentieth year of the reign of James I. in which the voters for members of Parliament are directed "not to choose curious and wrangling lawyers, who may seek reputation by stirring needless questions."

A strong prejudice was at this time, excited against lawyers. In Aleyn's "Henry VIII." (London, 1638) we have the following philippic against them:—

> "A prating lawyer, (one of those which cloud
>   That honour'd science), did their conduct take;
> He talk'd all law, and the tumultuous crowd
>   Thought it had been all gospel that he spake.
> At length, these fools their common error saw,
> A lawyer on their side, but not the law."

From Pierce Egan, Real life in London; or, The rambles and adventures of Bob Tallyho, esq. and ... Tom. Dashall, through the metropolis, by an amateur (1905), p. 246.

IV

THE LAWYER'S LIFE.

The lawyer having once enlisted in the service of Justice, the queen of all virtues, upon whom all other virtues wait as handmaids, strives that he may in all things approve himself a faithful follower of so good a mistress. And as without diligence all virtues do pine and languish, the lawyer's life is one of unwearied exertion; except at those times when the usage of his calling bids him rest awhile from his labours, and yield himself to the festive joys of the Christmas, or the soberer thoughts of the Easter season; or sends him to drink in bodily health and mental energy amid summer's delights. At other seasons, when clients demand not his time, he employs so much of it as is seasonable, in increasing his stores of legal knowledge, from whence as from a treasure-house to draw out sound counsel in time of need. When in health, he is ever at his post that he may not disappoint those who, confiding in his judgment and knowledge, are in the habit of entrusting him with the conduct of their affairs: and such principally he seeks not alone that they may with the more readiness disclose to him their whole case, but that he may with the more confidence rely on their integrity and veracity. His doors are ever open to the poor as well as to the rich; and though he knows well that labour is the lot of man and the labourer worthy of his hire, yet having proposed the holy name of Justice as the object of his labour's worship, he embraces as willingly the cause of the poor as of the rich, and strives no less earnestly for him who is unable to reward, than for him who is able and willing to reward him liberally. Yet he does not here forget the deceitfulness of the human heart, nor the eager love of gain which lies deep at its root.

He knows that here an enemy lurks, and he is ever on his guard against him; striving that not only in each individual case he may forget whether it be profitable to his purse or not, but that the whole tenor of his mind may be diverted from thoughts of gain. To this end he is careful so to order his affairs that his expenditure may be confined far within his income, lest want make him careless as to the means he employ to supply it. As in the affairs of others, by his counsel and his conduct, he dissuades them from seeking more than is their due; so, in his own affairs, he is exact to avoid even the appearance of evil; as knowing that for him to defeat in his own case the ends of justice by the forms of law, would not only bring twofold condemnation on himself, but subject him to solicitations to do the same for others. As business often brings him into converse and sometimes into co-operation with men of principles widely differing from his own; while he studies to be courteous to all, he is careful that he be not led by the suggestions or example of others to countenance what he himself disapproves: and when practices are proposed to him by which justice, truth, and honour would be wounded, if youth commands from him diffidence and distrust, he dissents with modesty yet firmness; if age gives him the liberty of rebuke, he censures with warmth and energy. Surrounded from the nature of his calling by evil, and forced to be ever and anon a witness to the workings of the bad passions of our nature, he relies not on his own strength alone to bear him unscathed amid the tempest that surrounds him, but ever as returning morn summons him to his daily task, he breathes forth an especial prayer to the Giver of all good that the labours of the day may be of justice, mercy, and truth, serving to the glory of God and the good of his fellow men; and whenever in the providence of God he has been made the means of succouring the oppressed, or by prudent management of relieving those distressed as to their worldly affairs, he takes not to himself the praise, but gives glory to Him from whom all power descends, to whom all praise is due.

From Edward O'Brien, *The Lawyer, His Character and Holy Rule of Life: After the Manner of George Herbert's Country Parson* (Philadelphia: Carey & Hart, 1843), pp. 25–26.

V

The great advantages which the world receives from the labours of eminent and learned men, are not so generally acknowledged as they ought to be. In our pursuit of literary knowledge, we seldom stop to reflect on the means whereby we are enabled to attain it. The chronologer, the annalist, the dictionary maker, though men of infinite labour, and some genius must not expect their reward in that sort of gratitude which contributes to their fame; nay, must be content to be considered as the drudges and pioneers of literature, to smooth the way for others. Nor does it fare much better with translators; in this case, the original author engrosses the whole applause. A man read the translation with advantage and pleasure; but thinks the commonwealth of letters no more indebted to the person who introduced it into the language, than to the printer who printed, or to the bookseller who sells the book.

From John Walker, LL.B., A Selection of Curious Articles from the Gentleman's Magazine, 3rd edition, vol. 2 (1814), p. 152.

VI

THE ANTIQUITY OF THE LAWS OF THIS ISLAND

by W. HAKEWILL

The antiquity of laws may be considered, either in respect of the ancient grounds, from whence they have been derived, or from the long time, during which they have been used within the same state or kingdom, of which the question is put. In both which respects, although perhaps the lawes of this island may justly be compared with any other in the Christian world, as first in regard of their long continuance within this land, but especially for that they agree with the written law of God, the law of primary reason, and the old laws of Greece (of all lawes humane the most ancient) in very many points, and those also, wherein they differ from the laws of other nations; yet because the meaning of the question in hand doth (as I conceive it) more properly bind me to say my opinion touching their continuance within this Island, bending myself only thereunto, I will purposely omit that other point of their derivation. And herein I will labour rather to find out the simple and plain truth, than seek to maintain any opinion heretofore conceived touching their very great antiquity; howsoever perhaps it may pretend more honor to our nation. Fortescue, Chancellour of England, in the dayes of H.6. in his treatise in praise of the laws of England, touching this matter hath these words:

> *Regnum Angliae primo per Britannos inhabitatum est, deinde per Romanos regulatum, iterumque per Britannos, ac deinde per Saxones possessum, qui nomen ejus ex Britannia in Angliae mutaverunt; ex tunc per Dacos idem regnum parumper dominatum est, & iterum per Saxones, sed finaliter per Normannos, quorum*

propago regnum illud obtinet in praesenti. Et in omnibus nationum
harum & Regum eorum temporibus regnum illud iisdem, quibus
jam regitur, consuetudinibus continue regulatum est.

For which opinion of his, because I see no other proof than
ipse dixit, though indeed the authority of the writer be great,
and the opinion such, as for the honor of our laws I could
willingly embrace; yet there being (as I conceive it) many
and those sound reasons, which prove the contrarie, I may
justly suppose, that the great affection, which he bore to the
profession, which had brought him to so high a place in the
common wealth, might move him in honor thereof to say
more than his best learning could otherwise inable him to
maintain. His authority, or perhaps the same motive hath
drawn some late writers also to publish the same opinion,
the which for my part I do not see any way maintainable,
but am rather of opinion, that the laws of the Britaines were
utterly extinct by the Romans; their laws again by the Saxons;
and lastly, theirs by the Danes and Normans much altered.

And first touching the Romans, who were the first,
that conquered the ancient inhabitants of this island:
considering, that it was their use alwayes to alter the laws
of those nations which they subdued, as even at this day
may appear in France, Spain, Germany, and many other
nations, and that in nothing more than this they placed the
honor and safety of their conquests, it is very likely, that
they also took the like course in this Island, which they did
in their other provinces; and indeed more reason had they
so to do here, than perhaps any where else in the whole
Empire, as being a province so farr remote, and a people
even by nature disobedient. To this may be added, that
they trained up some of the British kings and many of their
noblemen even in the city of Rome itself, which they did for
no other purpose, than to instruct them in their laws and
civilitie. Besides these probabilities, (which yet are of force

enough against a bare affirmation only of the contrary) there wanteth not also authority, which may prove the same; for even by the best authors and writers of the history of those times it is reported, that Vespasian coming hither in person, as lieutenant to Claudius, after the great victorie which he had obtained against Arviragus in the North parts, for the better assurance of his loyalty in time to come, and the more absolute subjection of the Britains for ever after, abrogated their ancient laws, and established those of the empire in their place. To this may be added the sending hither of the great Lawyer Papinian, only to reform the laws here; appointing in every several province a Roman judge to do justice accordingly. Neither is it a small argument hereof, that in part of this island itself, manely in Scotland, much of the civil law is even at this day in practice; the bringing of which among them can be assigned to no other time or persons, than to the old Romans, when they ruled this island. In proof whereof the Scottish chronicles do report, that Julius Caesar built a judgement hall in those parts near the city of Camelon, the ruines whereof remain at this day, and are called *Julius Hoffe,* or *Julius Hall.* If then in the space of forty or fifty years, during which time and no longer the Roman government continued in that country, being also alwayes rebellious, and for that came so soon forsaken by them, the Romans did so alter the laws there, that even to this day many of the laws, which they then established, do yet remain; it is more than probable, that they holding this part of the island above 400 years, and that in reasonable good peace, did also alter the laws here; especially considering, how easily this course, of so great consequence unto them, was to be continued, which by Vespasian, as before is said, was begun perhaps with much difficultie and resistance.

The next, that succeeded the Romans in conquest, were the Saxons, by whom so absolute and victorious a conquest was made of this land, as the like (I believe) in any history is scarce read of. For they did not only expel or drive into corners of the land the ancient inhabitants, planting themselves in their feats, and that not by small colonies, but as it were by whole nations of people; a point even in great conquests rarely heard of: but they altered also the religion, they razed out the old names of cities, towns, rivers, and whole countries, imposing new of their own invention; nay, the language itself they not only altered, but utterly abolished; and for a perfect consummation of their conquest they did at last also change the name of the whole island itself: than which, if there were no other argument proving the same, this methinks might very much persuade, that those great conquerors altered also the old laws, and established their own; than which as nothing is more of conquerors desired, and more usually put in practice; so indeed is there nothing of more honor and security in ages to come, if once it may be thoroughly performed; which how easy it was for the Saxons to bring to pass, when all the old inhabitants were either slain, fled out of the land, or run into the corners thereof, any man may judge; nay, expect those among the Saxons, which bore rule over the rest, would have enforced upon their own country-men the execution of a law strange unto them, the law of the Britaines their vanquisht enemies, than which nothing is more unlikely, it must needs follow, that the laws of the old Britaines did altogether cease in England amongst the Saxons; for that amongst them there were no other than Saxons, by whom the old British laws might have been executed. Of which the absolute ceasing of the British tongue here in England, and that in so short a space, if there were no other argument, is proof infallible.

But with this that hath been said, when we consider the long and prosperous reign, which the Saxons had in this island, the continual enmity between them and the

Britaines, and lastly their divided government requiring other laws, than those which were convenient for the entire monarchy; me thinks, little doubt should be made, but that the British laws were by them altered and their own brought in their place. To conclude this point; there are divers of the laws of the Saxon Kings extant among us at this day in their original tongue; there are also extant the British laws collected and confirmed by Howel Dah, or Howel the *good*, who ruled in Wales about A. 914. These laws being compared, the one with the other, do in the fundamental points so mainly differ, as scarce the laws of two nations in the world differ more.

Neither is it of small moment to this purpose, that the customes of little Britaine, whether many of the old Britaines fled, do also so much differ from the Saxon laws, and yet in so many points agree with those of Howel Dah; so as notwithstanding any opinion to the contrary, I make no doubt, but the Roman law, whereof without doubt much remained to the time of the Saxons, but much mingled with the British, as also the British law itself, were by the Saxons as utterly abolished, as if none such had ever been planted. And this absolute and almost admirable conquest of the Saxons, altering and turning all things upside down in this kingdom, is (as I conceive) the true and only reason, why less of the civil Law remaineth in this kingdom than in any other of the Roman Provinces at this day. For in all other nations of Europe the Roman bondage was cast off, either by revolt of the ancient inhabitants, who had lived long under the Roman laws and had by time approved them, or by invasion of some foreign nation, though perhaps as great enemies to the Roman government, as were the Saxons, yet not so wastefull and destroying, or perhaps in the conquests not so powerfull or fortunate as they. For only in this nation through the cruelty of the conquerors none of the inhabitants were left to be mingled with them, who might have been able to have preserved so much, as the fundamental points of the British or Roman laws.

Now as touching the Danes, though by reason, that their dominion within this island lasted but a very short space, they could not so much alter the laws of the Saxons, as before their time the Romans and Saxons had done the laws, which they found in this land, at the time of their several conquests; yet surely they also did much alter the Saxon laws, and brought into this land many of the laws of Denmark in their place, which even at this day remain amongst us. That so they did, besides many probabilities thereof, may appear by the difference, which we find by comparison between the laws of Canutus the Dane, and of the Saxon kings before him; as also by that, which by the consent of so many good and ancient Authors is reported of Edward the Confessor; namely, that he collected those laws of his, so much commended, amongst others, out of the Dane law: which without doubt he would not have done, being the aw of his mortal enemies, and a badge of their conquest, had not the Dane law been before his dayes planted in the realme, and received also of the people. But that which most moveth me, to think, that the Danes made a great alteration of our laws here, is the great agreement of our present common laws with the laws and customes of the Normans at this day; who, though they were called by a different or more general name of *Normans* or *Northmen*, and not by the more particular name of *Danes*, as were those which conquered England; yet did they, as all the writers of their history affirm, issue out of one and the same country, and were as much *Danes* as they. They also came out of Denmark to their several conquests of England and Normandy, within 3 or 4 years, the one of the other; namely, about the year of Christ 800; where having lived under one and the same law, and being therein bred and brought up, they did in their several conquests establish the same; and this is the true reason, as I conceive it, of the great affinitie of our laws with the customs of Normandy; in confirmation of which, the agreement of our common law with the laws of Denmark in fundamental points, wherein it differeth from the laws of all the world else, is also a great persuasion, namely in descents of inheritance and tryals of rights. For that the inheritance in Denmark was to the eldest, as in England, it may appear by the testimonie of Walsingham in his *Ypodigma Neustriae,* where he not only affirmeth the same, but alledgeth also the reason of the law herein in these words:

> *Mos erat in Dacia, cum replete esset terra hominibus, ut sancita lege per Reges illius terrae, cogerentur minores de propriis sedibus emigrare. Qua gens idcirca multiplicabatur nimium, quia luxui excessive dedita multis mulieribus jungebatur. Nam pater adultos filios cunctos a se pellebat, prater unum, quem heredem sui juris relinquebat.*

And indeed this manner of sole inheritance is with great good reason still upheld rather in these North parts, than in the more Southern countries of the world; where by reason their women are not fruitful as here, the inheritance is not divided into so many small parts, as here it would be, if the law of equal partition did prevail. Now as touching the trial also of rights in Denmark agreeable to that of England by 12. men, Olaus Magnus hath these words, ch. 21. *Expurgatio in judicio duodecim legalium hominum per Gothos in Italia degentes vetusto tempore observabatur, & hodierno die in Gothicis regnis observatur.* That the same form of trial and many other points also of our present laws, as our Tenures, wardships, dower of the thierd part, fines, and the like, were used here in England before the Conquest by the Normans, the proofes are very many, the which also shall little need; considering, that all the writers agree, that Henry the first did again restore the laws of Edward the Confessor, which by his father the Conqueror and by his brother before him had been somewhat altered, and that the fame doth also appear by his letters patents thereof, which are by Matthew of Paris recorded in his history. So as I am of opinion, (wherein nevertheless I do alwais submit mee to better judgement) that the British laws were altered by the Romans; theirs by the Saxons; and theirs again much altered by the Danes, which mingled with some points of the Saxon law, and fewer of the Norman law, is the common law now in use.

Nº II

OF THE ANTIQUITY OF THE LAWS OF ENGLAND

Mr. Attorney General in his third report hath made a very learned discourse of the antiquity of the laws of England, wherein he maketh mention of British laws, amongst the which some were called *Statuta municipalia*, and the others *leges judiciariae*; which is as much as to say, the *statute lawes*, and *the common laws*. But of those laws at this day I think there remaineth few or none, except they were preserved among the Britons, that fled into Wales: for the Saxons having made a full conquest, did alter as well the laws as the language; and in the beginning were a nation very rude and barbarous, as appeareth by their coynes, which I have ready to be shewed. For although they had the Roman coyn for a pattern, yet it seemeth, they regarded not any former precedents; but only such as were devised by themselves; and so do I think, they did of their laws; but after, when they became civil, they ordained many very good laws, whereof Mr. Lambert, that learned antiquary, hath caused a book to be printed, translated out of Saxon into Latin; but many of them, in my opinion, are very difficult to be understood; as among the laws of King Athelstone it is set down, that if any man shall kill another, he shall pay the whole value of his life, and the king's life is valued at 30000. thrimses; an archbishop is valued at 15000. thrimses; a bishop or a senator at 8000. thrimses; and so forth for every degree; and every thrimse was a coyne of the value of 3$^{sh.}$ And there also is set down, that King H. I. did value the life of any citizen of London at v$^{lib.}$ by his letters patents under the great seal; but in what order or unto whom this should be paid, it doth not there appear.

Also their ordinary laws are obscurely set down; for I have brought a piece of a charter of king Cenulfus, where it is said, *si malus homo tribus vicibus in peccatis suis deprehensus fuerit, ad regale vicum restituatur ad puniend.* but what the punishment should be, it doth not appear.

Also they made leases for three lives in those dayes, but somewhat differing in the terms from ours at this day; for I have a Saxon charter, whereby there is granted *terram quatuor manentium pro diebus trium hominum,* which was for three lives, as the use is at this day. The manner of their livery of seisin did in some cases differ for the use in our time; for I have a deed, whereby lands were given unto the priory of Cuic in Devon, whereunto there are many witnesses; but in the end there are these words, & *videntibus istis testibus, posui super altare sancti Andrea de Cuic per unum cultellum.* And Mr. Stow hath set down, that in the beginning of William the Conqueror's reign, farms and mannors were given by words without writing; only by delivery of the sword of the lord, or his head piece, by a bow or an arrow, and such like.

Also for the manner of out-lawries in those dayes; if any man had broken the peace of the Church violently, he was in the jurisdiction of the bishops to have justice; but if the party fled from it, the king by the words of his own mouth shall out-law him; and if after he may be found, he shall be delivered unto the King alive, or else his head, if he defend himself; for he beareth the head of a wolfe.

In the book of Domesday there is mention made of trial by Peers; the words are there, *Willielmus de Percye advocat Pares suos in testimonium, quod vivente Willielmo Mallet & vicecomitatum tenente in Everwick, ipse fuit seisitus de Bodetun, & eam tenuit:* and thus much for this time shall suffice.

Extract from Thomas Hearne, A Collection of Curious Discourses (London, 1771), pp. 1–11.

VII

... [He] labored incessantly to impress upon my mind the inutility of virtue, and the necessity of deception and hypocrisy, to a man destined as I was for the profession of the law. It was of no consequence, he said, whether the conduct of a lawyer were strictly consistent with the principles of integrity or not, for he would not, on that account, be more generally esteemed or more eminently conspicuous at the bar. The possession of wealth, he taught me to regard as the *opus magnum* of human life, and to obtain it, every faculty, both of body and mind, should be exerted, and every practice resorted to, however mean and contemptible, that would, in the smallest degree, contribute to the accomplishment of that end.

From S. Watterston, The Lawyer or Man as He Ought Not to Be (1808), pp. 13-14.

VIII

Lawyers familiarize to their minds the notion, that whatever is legally right is right; and when they have once habituated themselves to sacrifice the manifest dictates of equity to law, where shall they stop?

From J. Dymond, Essays on the Principles of Morality, and on the Private and Political Rights and Obligations of Mankind (1834), p. 156.

The

Austin Law Club

PARKER HOUSE

Friday, - - - April 21, 1893

-- MENU --

Bluepoints on Deep Shell

.... SOUPS ....

Mock Turtle   Consommé à la Royal

Radishes

.... FISH ....

Broiled Shad and Roe, Maître d'Hôtel

Potato Croquettes

.... REMOVES ....

Spring Lamb, Mint Sauce

Fillet of Beef, Mushrooms

Boiled Philadelphia Chicken, Purée of Spinach

.... ENTREES ....

Chicken Croquettes, with Peas

Vol au Vent of Lobster, à la Newburg

Fried Bananas, Glacé au Kirsch

. . . . SWEETS . . . .

Omelette Soufflée   Wine Jelly

Strawberry Short-Cake   Frozen Pudding

———

. . . . DESSERT . . . .

Oranges   Bananas   Apples   Strawberries

Nuts and Raisins

———

Ice Cream   Sherbet

———

Coffee

From a menu in the author's possession. The Austin Law Club was a Harvard Law School social club. Parker House was one of the most famous—and elegant—restaurants in nineteenth century Boston. The idea of lawyers and law students gathering for celebratory dinners is as old as the Anglo-American legal profession since group dinners were one of the primary social activities of the Inns of Court.

X

W— was wont to imbibe. On a certain occasion the duty laid upon him of arguing a *certiorari*. He had, prior to coming into court, partaken of a favorite drink and when he attempted to rise from his seat for the purpose of commencing his motion found the gravity of his body rather too great to overcome; but after repeated trials he at last gained his feet. The presiding judge discovering his situation and inability to express himself understandingly, said to him—

"Mr. W—, sit down; you are drunk."

To which remark W— slowly replied–

"That's a fact, and it's the first correct decision your honor has made this term."

From Charles Edwards, Pleasantries about Courts and Lawyers of the State of New York (New York, 1907), p. 122.

XI

Read *v.* Legard was an action brought for necessaries supplied to the defendant's wife at a time when he was confined in an asylum as a dangerous lunatic. In the course of the argument, Alderson B. inquired of the plaintiff's counsel if they should not apply to the Court of Chancery for relief. They replied: "While the grass is growing, the steed starves; while the Court of Chancery is deciding the cause, the woman might starve." The court decided that the action could be maintained.[1]

[1] 15 Jur. 494. See Shaw *v.* Thompson, 16 Pick. 198, 200.

* * *

Lord Mansfield, while confessing a wish for popularity, added, in words which cannot be too often quoted, "But it is that popularity which follows, not that which is run after; it is that popularity which, sooner or later, never fails to do justice to the pursuit of noble ends by noble means."

From Franklin Fiske Heard, Curiosities of the Law Reporters (Boston, 1871), pp. 26, 43.

XII

The studies by which a man may gain the summit of legal excellence are infinitely varied: he must possess the most opposite qualities, and be capable of exercising them; he must have a quick discernment, and yet a steady understanding; he must not be destitute of imagination, yet must he possess a sound judgment; he must know books, yet be well learned in mankind; the subtle technicality of law, and the enlarged beauties of classical learning; the solitary habits of study and the easy refinements of active life must equally distinguish him. In fine, he must unite in himself all those noble and useful qualities, by which he may at once command the attention of the acute and the learned, and render himself intelligible to the most ordinary capacity. Let him remember that every eye is busy in the discovery of his weaknesses, that every ear is open to the detection of his errors.

What a field is here for exertion! and yet I have presented you but with a hasty and imperfect sketch of the arduous task you are about to undertake. But our correspondence is not confined to strict and formal rules. What is omitted, or but slightly touched upon at one time, may be more particularly discussed at another; and at this entrance upon it, I have no other intention than to present to you a view of general principles. Accompany me with patience, and we will in time descend and apply these principles to particular propositions.

He who has not a mind susceptible of the habits of labour, or willing to acquire them, will never succeed at the bar: if such a man should entertain a design of studying the law, I would advise him to lay it aside. I have before said that I do not mean to alarm you; but it would be a sorry proof of friendship to deceive you with a false representation of things. I know how pleasing it is to the young mind to have ease and honour presented to it; but the combination, if not unnatural, is at least a very rare one; and the hope of meeting with it ought never to be indulged. To attain to an eminence in the law, is to attain to a great honour! the labour, therefore, must be proportionate.

From J. Raithby, The Study and Practice of the Law (Portland, 1806), pp. 44–45.

XIII

A lawyer sat idly in his chair
    (As lawyers sometimes do),
Discussing with a learned air
    A recent Code Review;
His auditors, some twelve or more
    Old barristers, sat near,
Each stuffed with pride and legal lore,
    With countenance austere.

The while these astute Solons sat,
    It chanced a client came
Whose presence stopped their social chat–
    A crabbed spinster dame.
"These are my brothers in Law, you see"
    Said Smythe, as she passed through;
"For goodness' sake, poor man!" cried she,
    "How many sisters have you?"

                –Jean La Rue Burnett

A lawyer quite famous for making a bill,
    And who in good living delighted,
To dinner one day with hearty good will
    By a rich client was invited.
But he charged six and eight pence on going to dine,
    Which the client he paid, though no ninny,
And in turn charged the lawyer for dinner and wine,
    One a crown and the other a guinea.
But gossips, you know, have a saying in store,
He who matches a lawyer has only one more.

The lawyer he paid and took a receipt,
     While the client stared at him with wonder;
With the produce he gave a magnificent treat,
     But the lawyer soon made him knock under.
That his client sold wine, information he laid,
     Without license, and in spite of his storming
The client a good thumping penalty paid,
     And the lawyer got half for informing.
But gossips, you know, have a saying in store,
He who matches a lawyer has only one more.

*From William C. Sprague, Flashes of Wit from
Bench and Bar (Detroit, 1895), pp. 49, 182.*

XIV

HONEST LAWYERS.

To prove that lawyers honest are
In vain alas you try
While truth may be within their words
Their *actions* always *lie*.

From Edward R. Johnes, *Briefs by a Barrister*
(New York, 1879).

XV

ON THE STUDY OF THE LAW.

Every gentle man ought to know a little of law, says Coke, and perhaps, say we, the less the better. Servius Sulpicius, a patrician, called on Mutius Scaevola, the Roman Pollock (not one of the firm of Castor and Pollux), for a legal opinion, when Mutius Scaevola thoroughly flabbergasted Servius Sulpicius with a flood of technicalities, which the latter could not understand. Upon this Mutius Scaevola bullied his client for his ignorance; when Sulpicius, in a fit of pique, went home and studied the law with such effect, that he wrote one-hundred-and fourscore volumes of law books before he died; which task was, for what we know, the death of him. We should be sorry, on the strength of this little anecdote, to recommend our nobility to go home and write law books; but we advise them to peruse the Comic Blackstone, which would have done Servius Sulpicius a great deal of good to have studied.

The clergy and the Druidical priests were in former times great lawyers; and the word *clericus* has been corrupted into clerks, so that the seedy gentlemen who carry the wigs and gowns down to court for the barristers are descended from the Druids.

A contest sprung up between the nobles and clergy, the former supporting the common law, and the other the civil. Somebody having picked up a copy of the pandects of Justinian at a book-stall in Amalfi introduced them into England, but King Stephen would not allow them to be studied. Roger Vacarius, however, set up an evening academy for adults, where he advertised to teach the pandects on moderate terms; but the laity would not come to his school at any price. One thing that contributed to save the common law from falling into disuse was the fixing of the Court of Common Pleas, which had formerly been moveable, following the person of the king, like Algar's booth or Richardson's show, with all the paraphernalia of a Court of Justice. It is probable that the Common Pleas had a van to carry the barristers' bench, the judge's easy chair, and the rostrum for the witnesses, from place to place; but when it became fixed, it made it worth the while of respectable people to study the law, which was not the case when the legal profession was nothing but a strolling company.

To those who take up the study of the law for the mere fun of the thing, we say with Sir John Fortescue, "It will not," &c &c., down to "other improvements."

From The Comic Blackstone (London, 1846), pp. 1-2.

XVI

Take, for instance, the Lawyer. It is Saturday night.—Court has adjourned late. He returns home weary and exhausted in body and mind. He seats himself in his office.—"To what purpose all this labor and weariness and anxiety? What real advantage do I hope to derive from all these struggles and projects and speculations? Suppose I acquire wealth and reputation, can they make me happy? Alas! I am weary of them even now. I know and feel, that this soul of mine was created for nobler purposes. My possessions too I must soon leave. Leave? — and where shall I then go? To a world for which I have made no preparation. — To a world of disembodied spirits, where nothing of all that I value here will be of the least use to me. Why then this labor and anxiety? What folly! What madness! Why not at once follow the dictates of reason and common sense, and begin to live for something better?"

From Anonymous, A Few Thoughts by a member of the Bar (New Haven, 1836), pp. 49–50.